Katie
LET'S CELEBRATE

# Take Time

## A MOTHER'S JOURNAL

sourcebooks
eXplore

To my grandmothers, Marie and Clarice.
*You taught me to be brave in order to begin.*

Niklas's art, age 6

Copyright © 2020 by Katie Clemons LLC
Cover and internal design © 2020 by Sourcebooks
Cover art by Connie Gabbert
Internal art © MG Drachal/Shutterstock, LudaRu/Shutterstock, Olena Yepifanova/Getty Images, Ekaterina Romanova/Gett Images, Toltemara/Getty Images, Aluna1/Getty Images, BOTOBOX/Getty Images, mari_matayoshi/Getty Images, ruslana_newsom/Getty Images, Hulinska_Yevheniia/Getty Images, ulimi/Getty Images, frimages/Getty Images, Anatartan/Getty Images, AllNikArt/Getty Images, SlyBrowney/Getty Images, Designed by pikisuperstar/Freepik, Designed by Freepik, Designed by BiZkettE1/Freepik, Designed by rocketpixel/Freepik, rawpixel.com

Published by Sourcebooks eXplore, an imprint of Sourcebooks Kids
P.O. Box 4410, Naperville, Illinois 60567-4410
(630) 961-3900
sourcebooks.com

Printed and bound in the United States of America.
VP 10 9 8 7 6 5 4 3 2 1

# The moments matter

**SATURDAY MORNING IS MY KIND OF MORNING.** My kids and I tie on handmade aprons. We gather bowls and measuring cups and start beating a few eggs. Together we make the most amazing blueberry pancakes with dollops of yogurt, maple syrup, and fresh nutmeg.

I live for moments like these with my kids, though I suspect we will never find a Norman-Rockwellesque picture of our process. I ping-pong across the kitchen to maintain progress and squelch chaos. I try to remind five-year-old Niklas not to let his egg-smeared whisk fall on the floor, but he's distracted. *Plunk.* Two-year-old Linden adds a cup of flour before we're ready, and—*poof*—a plume of dust rises over the counter.

I step back and take a quick gulp of hot tea. It's all I can do before diving back into the confusion.

Niklas is confident he can add the next egg alone. *Crack.* We only fish out a few shells. I can't recall if we added baking powder, so I measure a spoonful. Meanwhile Linden is ready to eat. He pulls open the deep drawer where we keep his plates. *Bam!* My shins were in the way.

I limp backward and gulp more tea.

I could have made breakfast alone. We could've eaten cold cereal. Heck, it's the weekend—we could've gone out for breakfast! But our clamorous morning ritual is a moment where I thrive as a mom. Not distracted by never-ending to-do lists and obligations, I take time to be completely present—to *breathe in, breathe out*—and cherish the moments where I can show my kids love and be loved in return.

Over the years, I have learned—as have countless moms—that in order to be the best version of ourselves, we also have to care for ourselves. And making that happen can be more difficult than getting any breakfast on the table.

Motherhood is an expedition that swings between utter exhaustion and exhilaration; it changes us and makes us better. But the litany of demands can also cause us to lose who we are. Instead of taking time to restore ourselves, we often push harder. We fill every nook of time with responsibilities. We take care of everything for everyone...except ourselves.

Thankfully I have found that keeping a journal is both the easiest and most powerful way to pause and nurture yourself. Journaling helps you explore personal interests, rest your body, and remember who you are deep inside. The solitude of writing gives you an opportunity to relax, appreciate life's gifts, and embrace the comfort of your own company. It's like savoring a cup of your favorite drink without someone begging for a sip.

"Hey, Mom!" Niklas says. He's waving the spatula toward me, a twinkle in his eyes and berry stains on his lips. "Is it time to cook the first pancake?"

"Yeah!" squeals Linden, and he lifts his plate as high as his flour-covered fingers can reach.

Our pancake griddle is hot, my abandoned tea is cold, and half of our blueberries have vanished. I smile, knowing the joy on my boys' faces will remain in my heart forever. "Let's get cooking!" I tell them.

In this journal, you'll find varying types of prompts. Some will make you chuckle as you reflect on times of get-out-the-door-to-school insanity, while others celebrate moments you wish you could live in forever. Keep these five guideposts in mind as you write. They'll help you make the most of this journal.

## 1. Take time to pursue solitude.

Uninterrupted moments of self-care, even brief ones, are precious gifts you can give yourself. This journal helps you focus inward during fragmented pockets of your day, with prompts that you can answer on the go. It also contains pages best worked during stretches of uninterrupted time.

I admit, I have journaled in the preschool coatroom. I've gone to appointments ten minutes early or neglected chores in order to have a few minutes to write. And more than once, I've tucked my journal in my bag and left my phone behind. My absolute favorite time to journal is early morning, when my mind feels rested and the house is silent. Throughout each day, I intentionally give myself permission to take time with my thoughts, and I want you to as well.

## 2. Take time to let your pen wander.

Give yourself permission to relinquish every notion you've assumed about journaling. A well-used, imperfect journal is infinitely better than an empty one. Write like you talk. Set a timer and journal until it dings. Start on the first page and work your way through, or flip to a prompt that intrigues you in the moment. Jot down a little or dive deep into a story.

I smudge ink and misspell words in my journal all the time. I've got entries that drop mid-sentence because nap time ended. Some of my pages get layered with toddler scribbles and swirls. Drinks get spilled. The phone rings. Sticky fingers flip through my pages. The pen disappears. I misplace my journal. These instances and a million more encapsulate mom life. Let's keep writing!

## 3. Take time to feel your emotions.

Use this journal to collect moments worth savoring. Fill it with as many hearts and "I love yous" as you fancy. Give yourself permission to write your way through how you're really feeling, especially when you need to face fear, claim your strength, or accept things you can't control. I know how taxing motherhood can feel, and it's scary to admit vulnerability and feelings of failure. Thankfully I've learned that writing can provide you with personal space to reflect and find your way through.

## 4. Take time to be creative.

Think of this journal as a creative outlet where *you* make all the rules. Write bubble letters like you did in elementary school. Doodle arrows and hearts. Tear pages out or tape more in. Color the illustrations. Draw speech boxes and emojis. Try your daughter's pens or your son's stickers. Scribble like a toddler. Use colored pencils and crayons. Snap pictures and collect keepsakes, then adhere them with glue or double-sided tape. More than anything, have fun!

## 5. Take time to go beyond these pages.

Your storycatching only begins with the pages of this journal. Come join me for exclusive *Take Time* resources, which include holiday pages you can print and add to your journal, easy-assembly projects to keep kids engaged while you write, and examples from my own journals online at:

KATIECLEMONS.COM/A/CM8K

I'd love to hear how your journal is coming together. Please drop me a note at **howdy@katieclemons.com** (I answer all my mail) or join me on social media **@katierclemons, #katieclemonsjournals,** and **#taketimejournal.**

Imagine the future keepsake this journal will be in ten or twenty years. Picking it up will transport you back in time as you flip through pages of stories that have long-since passed and see handwritten moments you'd forgotten, phrases you hadn't heard in years, photographs, illustrations, and best of all...reminders of how much you give love and are loved in return.

**You're a great mom.** Take time to pause, and... Let's celebrate your story!

♡ Katie

# Here's a photograph or drawing
## of me mothering

*A mother's love knows no limits.*

# Hello crazy, wonderful life!

The bigger my kids grow, the more my heart expands. This journal chronicles my joy and gratitude for this gift of being their mom, and it's a gentle nudge to myself to take time.

My name

My kids call me

My age and location

My kids' names and ages

Today's date

In my heart, I'm feeling

Here's how
## MY STORY UNFOLDS...

# I remember

the day I knew I was becoming a mom

DATE _____

# I'm so grateful

to have people who call me mom because

# Here's my whole gang!

## My people are

Our family theme song could be

People might guess we're related because

Some of the best things about my family are

1.

2.

3.

☐ I absolutely adore my people.

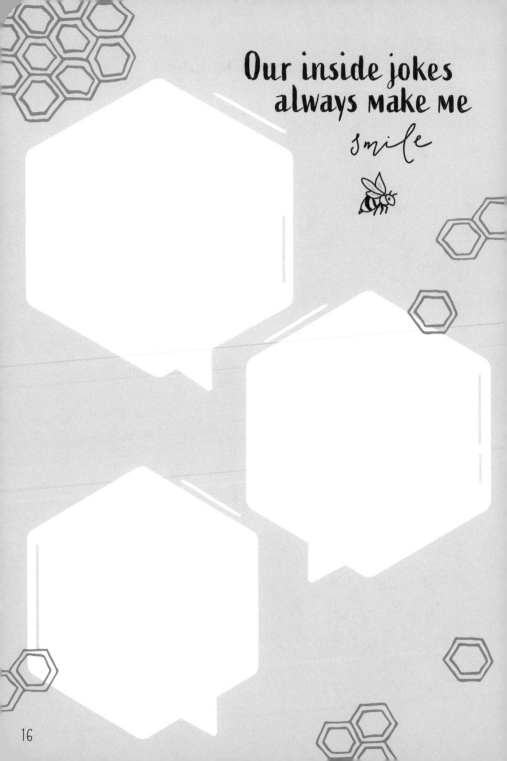

Our inside jokes
always make me
smile

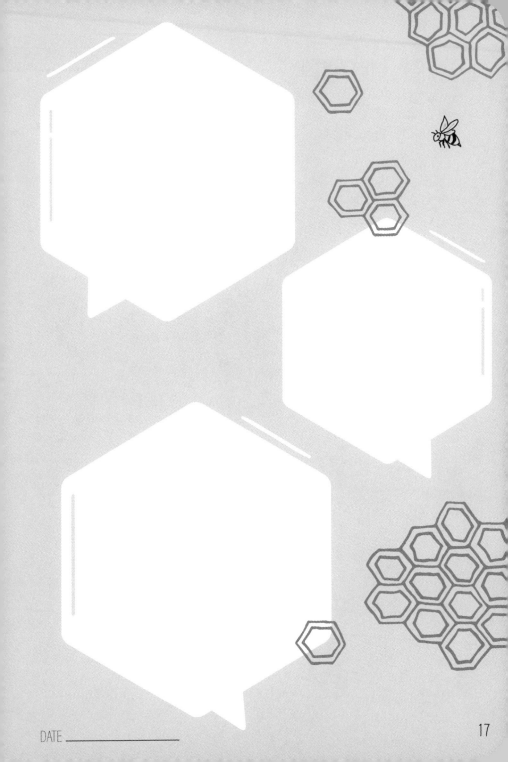

# Three things

My days are filled with

1.

2.

3.

I always have time for

1.

2.

3.

I never have time for

1.

2.

3.

DATE _____

# Here's a glimpse of me

In the morning

At the end of the day

When I'm home alone

When everyone's home

# Here's what I always tell my kids

# Me before kids

Here's what I want my kids to know about me

*The flowers of tomorrow started as seeds.*

# Cool things my family  has done together

1.

2.

3.

4.

5.

6.

DATE _____

# Amazing things we
## *still need to do* **together**

1.

2.

3.

4.

5.

6.

DATE _____

# Today I am
## feeling *thankful* for

DATE _____

# Sometimes I stay up *too late* at night because

And then I've got to be up at _____ o'clock to start the day.

# I want my family to have

Time for

Friends who

A home where

Lives that

DATE _____

# I want to have

### Time for

### Friends who

### A home where

### A life that

# We're fortunate to already have

### Time for

### Friends who

### A home where

### Lives that

DATE _____

# This is the *story of teeth* in this house

# I'm a proud mama today!

## Here's why

# Here's a photograph or drawing of our _____ home!

What I love most about our home is

Our favorite things to do here are

My bed often becomes a place where

A typical dinner scene looks like

Our average Monday morning sounds like

Love
*grows*
here.

# I tell my kids

It's okay to cry when

Stand up for yourself when

Try to keep going when

Be gentle and love yourself when

It's okay to ask for help when

Remember to forgive when

Be patient when

36

DATE _____

# I need to remind myself

It's okay to cry when
- - - - - - - - - - - - - - - - - - - - - - - - - -

Stand up for yourself when
- - - - - - - - - - - - - - - - - - - - - - - - - -

Try to keep going when
- - - - - - - - - - - - - - - - - - - - - - - - - -

Be gentle and love yourself when
- - - - - - - - - - - - - - - - - - - - - - - - - -

It's okay to ask for help when
- - - - - - - - - - - - - - - - - - - - - - - - - -

Remember to forgive when
- - - - - - - - - - - - - - - - - - - - - - - - - -

Be patient when
- - - - - - - - - - - - - - - - - - - - - - - - - -

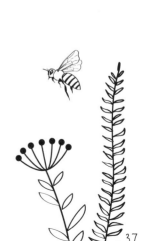

DATE _____

# Currently on my

Nightstand

_____

_____

Bucket list

_____

_____

To-do list

_____

_____

Dinner plate

_____

_____

Bedroom walls

_____

_____

Playlist

_____

_____

Mind

_____

_____

Web browser

_____

_____

Kitchen counter

_____

_____

Feet

_____

_____

Refrigerator shelves

_____

_____

Shopping list

_____

_____

_____

_____

_____

DATE _____

39

# I love being a MOM because

*The moments matter.*

# Today I am

Reading

_____

Watching

_____

Drinking

_____

Feeling

_____

Working on

_____

DATE _____

# When I take time for self-care in the morning

I drink
_____

I look at
_____

I quickly try to
_____

I leisurely take time to
_____

I try not to let myself
_____

One day, I'd like to
_____

DATE _____

43

# This I know

My family consumes incredible amounts of

We're constantly running out of

Someone's always forgetting _____

_____

_____

_____

I find myself laughing when _____

_____

_____

_____

I can trigger eye rolls whenever I _____

_____

_____

_____

I find myself regularly thinking

Someone is always saying

It's adorable when _____

_____

_____

_____

_____

Three words that describe us are

I give this _____ family ☆☆☆☆☆ stars!

DATE _____

# This is now

Our morning routine

Our bedtime routine

DATE _____

# My heart melted when

_____

_____

_____

_____

_____

_____

_____

_____

_____

_____

_____

_____

_____

_____

_____

_____

_____

_____

_____

_____

_____

_____

_____

_____

_____

_____

DATE _____

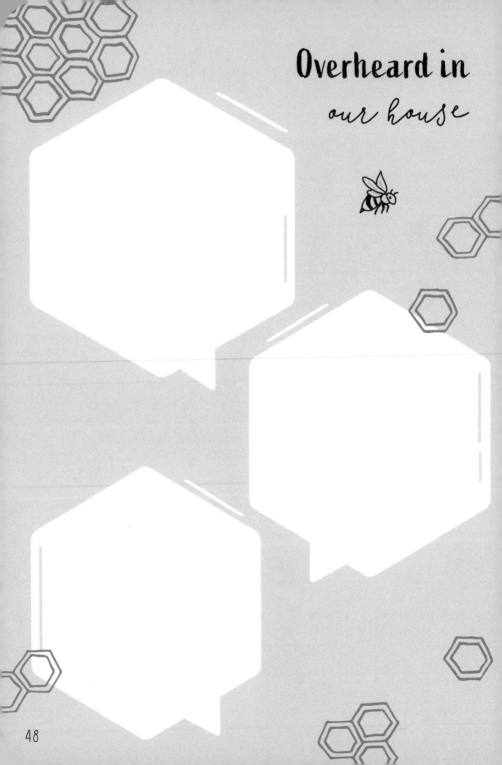

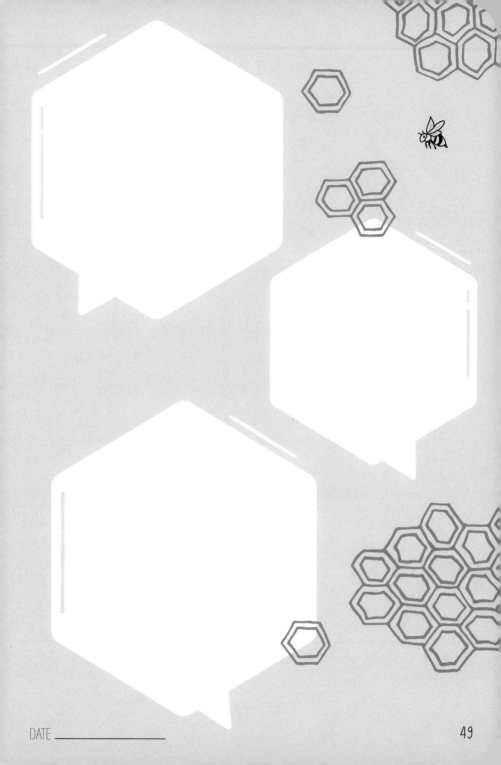

# This is me

Let your *heart* sing.

When I look at this picture, I feel

Two of my great traits that this picture shows

1.

2.

Two wonderful traits it doesn't reveal

1.

2.

# I'm always

CARRYING

WEARING

HELPING PEOPLE LOOK FOR

PICKING UP

# Movies, books, and shows
*my family loves*

# Movies, books, and shows
## I love

# My Typical Weekday

6:00 _____

7:00 _____

8:00 _____

9:00 _____

10:00 _____

11:00 _____

NOON _____

1:00 _____

2:00 _____

3:00 _____

4:00 _____

5:00 _____

6:00 _____

7:00 _____

8:00 _____

9:00 _____

10:00 _____

DATE _____

# My Typical Weekend

6:00 _____

7:00 _____

8:00 _____

9:00 _____

10:00 _____

11:00 _____

NOON _____

1:00 _____

2:00 _____

3:00 _____

4:00 _____

5:00 _____

6:00 _____

7:00 _____

8:00 _____

9:00 _____

10:00 _____

DATE _____

# Around here,

I'll always cherish these snuggles

DATE _____

# These are the people who support and cheer for me

# Hello today!

☐ Monday ☐ Tuesday ☐ Wednesday ☐ Thursday ☐ Friday ☐ Saturday ☐ Sunday

Today's schedule looks like

In three words, I feel like our day is

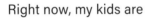

Right now, my kids are

Our house looks like

Dinner is

Our house smells like

Our house sounds like

We're planning

We're loving

We're NOT _____ ing!

One of my favorite moments has been

I give today ☆☆☆☆☆ stars!

# I never imagined that I would

---

*for another person*

DATE _____

# A typical breakfast scene around here

On a busy weekday morning

On a leisurely weekend morning

# Around here

On a scale of 1 to 5, I'm

BEING PATIENT WITH MYSELF ♡ ♡ ♡ ♡ ♡

EXPRESSING GRATITUDE TO OTHERS ♡ ♡ ♡ ♡ ♡

FEELING PROUD OF MY KIDS ♡ ♡ ♡ ♡ ♡

BEING OPEN-MINDED ♡ ♡ ♡ ♡ ♡

TAKING TIME TO BREATHE ♡ ♡ ♡ ♡ ♡

LISTENING TO MYSELF ♡ ♡ ♡ ♡ ♡

FEELING JOYFUL ♡ ♡ ♡ ♡ ♡

GETTING ENOUGH REST ♡ ♡ ♡ ♡ ♡

Reflections on my ratings

# My kids like to

Eat

Relax with

Play with

Ignore

Wear

Listen to

DATE _____

# I like to

Eat


Relax with


Play with


Ignore


Wear


Listen to

# People might guess I'm a MOM because

# What I always
## look forward to

Spring

Summer

Autumn

Winter

# Since becoming a MOM, these are *wonderful* ways

My priorities have changed

My schedule has changed

My home has changed

My body has changed

My relationships have changed

My _____ has changed

I have changed

# I never want to forget

a few details about my family right now

*Take time
for now.*

# My hopes for my family as we grow in the world

A year from now, I predict we

In five years, I imagine we

Hope blooms.

In twenty years, I hope we

# My favorite holiday is

The house smells like _____

_____

_____

_____

I love to decorate with _____

_____

_____

_____

One of my favorite traditions is _____

_____

_____

_____

I love these food rituals _____

_____

_____

_____

I try to make the season feel magical for my kids because _____

_____

_____

_____

I remember one time when _____

_____

_____

_____

## HERE'S US CELEBRATING!

# Around here

I'm really happy that
- - - - - - - - - - - - - - - - - -

I'm relieved that
- - - - - - - - - - - - - - - - - -

I worry about
- - - - - - - - - - - - - - -

I'm overwhelmed by
- - - - - - - - - - - - - - - - - - - -

I'm hopeful that

I'm wondering when

I'm confident that

I'm grateful for

# At our house

We can get dinner on the table in _____ minutes, which means we eat

a lot of _____

Our fridge is always full of _____

_____

_____

Our typical go-to dinners are

During the week, breakfast typically consists of _____

_____

_____

I want my kids to drink _____

_____ ☐ I do ☐ I don't drink it too.

I drink a lot of

☐ coffee ☐ tea ☐ soda ☐ water

☐ milk ☐ juice ☐ _____

I enjoy ☐ wine ☐ beer ☐ both ☐ neither

When no one else is home, I eat _____

and drink _____

I can sing all the words to

Because of this, my kids think that I am _____

_____

_____

They listen to a lot of _____

_____

which I think is _____

_____

In three words, I'd describe our home life as

I sound just like my mom when

Every day, I tell my kids

# Eight things that always make me happy

DATE _____

# Watching my children sleep feels like

# I'll always cherish

The sound of

_____

The smell of

_____

The taste of

_____

The sight of

_____

The feel of

_____

DATE _____

# Beautiful and brave things

that past generations of women in my family have done

# This is the story of *kid shoes* in this house

# At home

I always say no to
----------------------

I frequently say yes to
----------------------

I consistently forget
----------------------

I regularly remember
----------------------

DATE _____

# A love letter to my mom

and a thank-you for what she's taught me

DATE _____

# When it's *just me*

I enjoy time to


I would enjoy time to


I'm so glad I recently took time to

# What I cherish most

kindness

solitude

honesty

love

family

time

inner beauty

newness

wealth

adventure

naptime

achievement

generosity

familiarity

experiences

comfort

laughter

knowledge

connection

time

promptness

culture

faith

consciousness

gratitude

community

nature

courage

memories

certainty

hugs and kisses

equality

friendship

laughter

opportunity

appearance

passion

*Mark appropriate words*

stability

creativity

# Reflections
## ON THE WORDS I CHOSE

# A seasonal snapshot

Here's us right now

I enjoy this time of year because _____

_____

_____

It smells like                          It sounds like

_____              _____

_____              _____

It tastes like                          It looks like

_____              _____

_____              _____

It feels like

_____

When we're outside, my family _____

_____

_____

_____

When we're inside, we _____

_____

_____

_____

I remember one time when _____

_____

_____

_____

_____

_____

_____

_____

_____

_____

We give the season ☆☆☆☆☆ stars!

# Everyday things that make my kids happy

DATE _____

# Everyday things that
## make me *happy*

*Take time
to breathe.*

# I know I'm loved because

DATE _____

# This is my

EXCITED FACE

GOOFY FACE

EXHAUSTED FACE

CURIOUS FACE

FRUSTRATED FACE

IMPRESSED FACE

DATE _____

# These are the stories

of other adults who've impacted my kids' lives

# Lessons my kids have taught me about life

# Today I am

FEELING

ENJOYING

THINKING

COORDINATING

POSTPONING

HELPING

DATE _____

# Here's how we celebrate birthdays around here!

I try to make birthdays feel special in our family because

One of my favorite traditions is

I remember one time when

I love how my kids honored one of my recent birthdays by

# I'M ___ years into motherhood, and overall it's been

*Mark appropriate words*

exhausting

fulfilling

over-caffeinated

moving too fast

beautiful

amusing

breathtaking

tender

overwhelming

joyful

messy

pure magic

comedic

emotional

If I could slow down time

DATE _____

# Here's a *keepsake* from my life right now

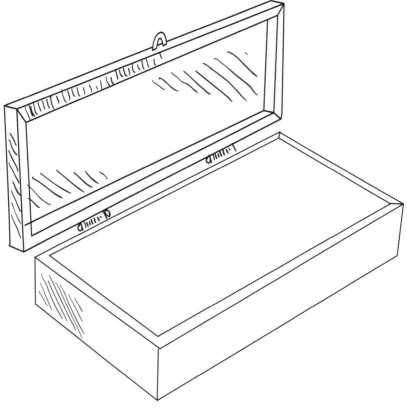

_____ Thing my kid made    _____ Reminder to myself

_____ Quote or poem    _____ Wrapper

_____ List or note from my bag    _____ Receipt

_____ Photo or picture    _____

I'm adding it to my journal because

# I remember when I held my child for the first time

Take time to
look back.

# I estimate

The number of shoes in this house

How many kids' books we own

The number of library books we've lost

The number of _____ in my purse

The quantity of cups of
coffee/tea/soda consumed daily here

The number of gallons of milk we buy weekly

The amount of cash in my wallet

How many cups we use in a single weekday

The number of laundry loads we wash each week

How many more hours of sleep I could use in a week

The number of hugs, high fives, and "I love yous"
happening in a single day here

_____

_____

DATE _____

I take time for
*myself* by

# This is the story of how we get
## food in this house

DATE _____

Today I am

Smiling about

_____

Guiltlessly neglecting

_____

Giving

_____

Expecting

_____

Appreciating

_____

# This is my *love letter* to our neighborhood

Here's a map or picture

*Find the beauty
in the everyday.*

# Around here today

Here's a picture

_____

is making me LOL

_____

is helpful

_____

is so fast

_____

has a heart of gold

_____

is being brave

_____

deserves a high five

DATE _____

# This is the story of

where (and how) kids sleep in this house

The first person asleep is usually _____

_____

_____

Our night owl tends to be _____

_____

_____

 And then in the morning _____

_____

_____

_____

_____

Our perky morning person is _____,

while _____would prefer to stay in bed.

And I'm _____

_____

_____

_____

_____

Give me all the ☐ coffee ☐ tea ☐ caffeine-free _____

☐ _____ to jumpstart my day.

# Here's a picture

of my family relishing a recent vacation

I give our trip ☆☆☆☆☆ stars!

☐ We loved our trip!

☐ Okay, getting there took kinda long.

☐ We could live there.

We ate and drank so much _____

_____

I got the chance to _____ alone!

We got to try _____

_____

We forgot to bring _____

_____

Our vacation theme song could have been _____

_____

The best parts of our trip were

1.

2.

3.

4.

5.

**LET'S GO BACK!**

# Before I became a mom

I thought a lot about
- - - - - - - - - - - - - - - - - - - - -

I spent a lot of time on
- - - - - - - - - - - - - - - - - - - - - -

I felt grateful for
- - - - - - - - - - - - - - - -

I felt confident about
- - - - - - - - - - - - - - - - - - - - - -

DATE _____

# As a mom

I think a lot about
- - - - - - - - - - - - - - - - - - - -

I spend a lot of time on
- - - - - - - - - - - - - - - - - - - - - - - -

I feel grateful for
- - - - - - - - - - - - - - - - - -

I feel confident about
- - - - - - - - - - - - - - - - - - - - - -

# My child made me a _____.
# I'll cherish it *forever* because

Here's a picture

DATE _____

# Dear Heart, it's okay to let go of

# Here's what I know about myself

I laugh when

I cry when

I sing when

I dance when

I push myself forward when

I'm a _____ mom.

DATE _____

# The best way to spend
## Saturday mornings

With my kids

When I was a kid

# A love letter to my body

*Love brews here.*
*Take time to care for yourself.*

# I remember a happy story
## from my childhood

DATE _____

# I'm grateful for this

Friend _____

Fellow parent _____

Daily ritual _____

Mantra _____

_____

Subscription _____

Cleaning tool _____

Relative _____

Parenting mentor or resource _____

_____

Technology _____

Kitchen gadget _____

Weather _____

Moment with my child _____

_____

# Here's a picture of
## *me and my kids*

*Take time to be present in this moment.*

Looking at this picture makes me feel

I think it captures our relationship well because

I feel like I radiate beauty in this picture because

I hope my kids know how much I

# A love letter to my children

You make me _____ everyday!

# Recent moments when I've felt

COMPOSED

CONFIDENT

CURIOUS

CONFLICTED

*Take time to follow your heart.*
*It knows the way.*

COURAGEOUS

COMPELLED

CONGRATULATORY

COMPLETELY EXHAUSTED!

I will cherish
these days forever

# Some things I've been
## *longing to do*

With my kids

By myself

DATE _____

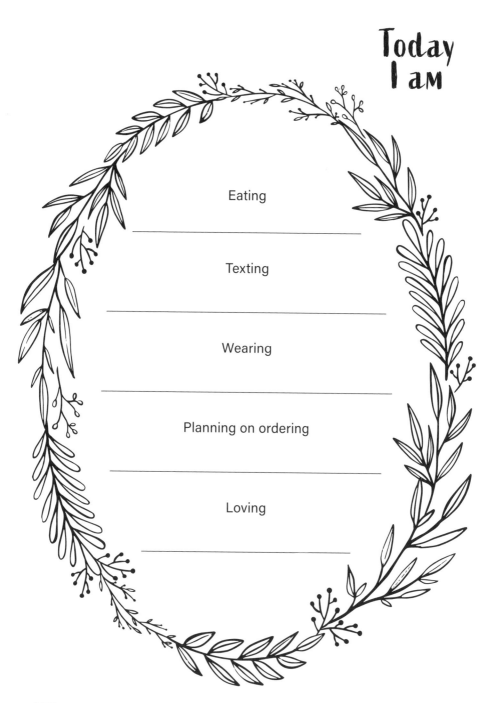

# Today I am

Eating

_____

Texting

_____

Wearing

_____

Planning on ordering

_____

Loving

_____

# *I try.* Sometimes I fail.

I want my kids to know about trying and failing, especially when they think they'll never achieve a dream, because I've been there. I'll be back many times, and I have learned that

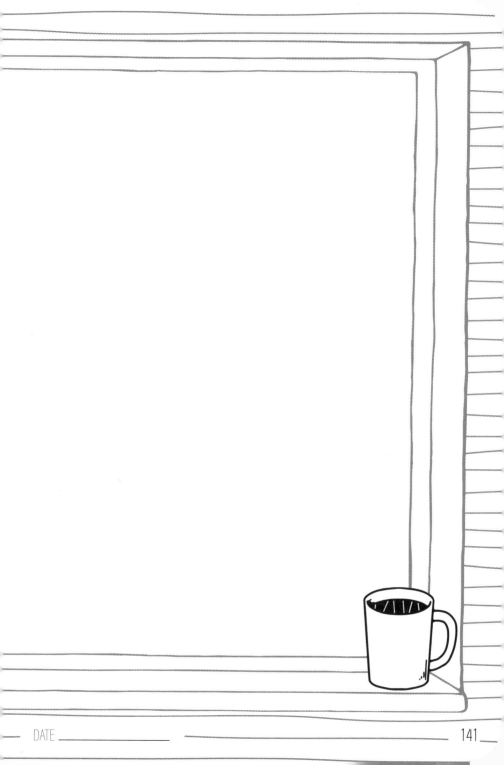

# A few last thoughts

before I finish this journal—my love letter to motherhood

DATE _____